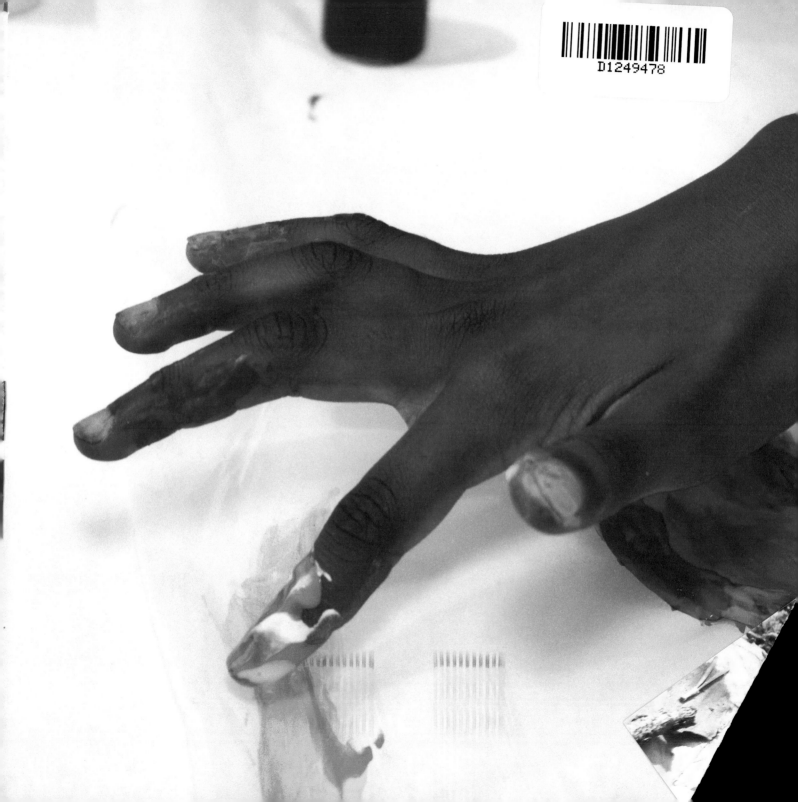

D1249478

6 C's for Creation Care

by Heidi Ferris

Other Growing Green Hearts books in this series:

- 1-2-3 Earth, Air & Me
- 4 S's for Noticing Nature: Senses, Sun, Systems, Seasons
- 5 R's for Environment: Rethink, Reduce, Reuse, Recycle, Rejoice*
- 6 C's for Creation Care: Creation, Christ, Creativity, Combustion, Climate, Connect*
- 7 Water Wonderings
- 8 Butterfly Questions for Gardening

Books that include science and faith together.

www.growinggreenhearts.com

Growing
Green Hearts

About This Series

This series of books, Playing with Science and Systems, has been created to be simple, scientifically accurate, and sometimes focused on faith. Science is problem finding and problem solving. The author Heidi Ferris is passionate about encouraging youth to ask questions, boosting science literacy, empowering kids to care for our shared resources, and exploring the wonders in God's creation. Heidi lives in Minnesota with her family - not far from the Mississippi River.

—

The brilliant blossoms and strong roots of blue flag iris work to create habitat and clean water by anchoring shorelines. This book is dedicated to those named Iris, both plants and people, who share beauty, grace, whimsy, and problem-solving skills with the world.

Copyright © 2016 Heidi Ferris, Growing Green Hearts LLC
Written and Edited by: Heidi Ferris
Graphic Design: Lisa Carlson, Spiira Design
Series Consultant: Janine Hanson, Janine Hanson Communications

All rights reserved. No part of this publication may be reproduced, stored in a retrieval system, or transmitted in any form or by any means, electronic, mechanical, photcopying, recording, or otherwise, without prior permission. For information regarding permission contact Growing Green Hearts LLC.

Available from Amazon.com and other retail outlets.

Contents

6 C's for Creation Care

6 Important C's in this book.

They are around us everyday,
we just forget to look.

1

C is for Creation.

God is the source of all things. People are to nurture and care for creation. Creation includes the air, water, land, and all living things.

C is for Christ.

Jesus Christ teaches about love and forgiveness.

2

Food Pantry Donations Needed

Sharing, helping, caring and listening are ways to spread love around.

9

3 C is for Creativity.

Creativity is when people share their ideas in different ways — movement, painting, building, cooking, singing, language, drawing, solving problems and more.

God made you as a special being.
How do you show your creativity?

4

C is for Combustion.

Combustion means to burn. People burn fuels when using electricity, driving cars, cooking food, and heating homes.

Combustion pollutes the air with heat-trapping gasses.

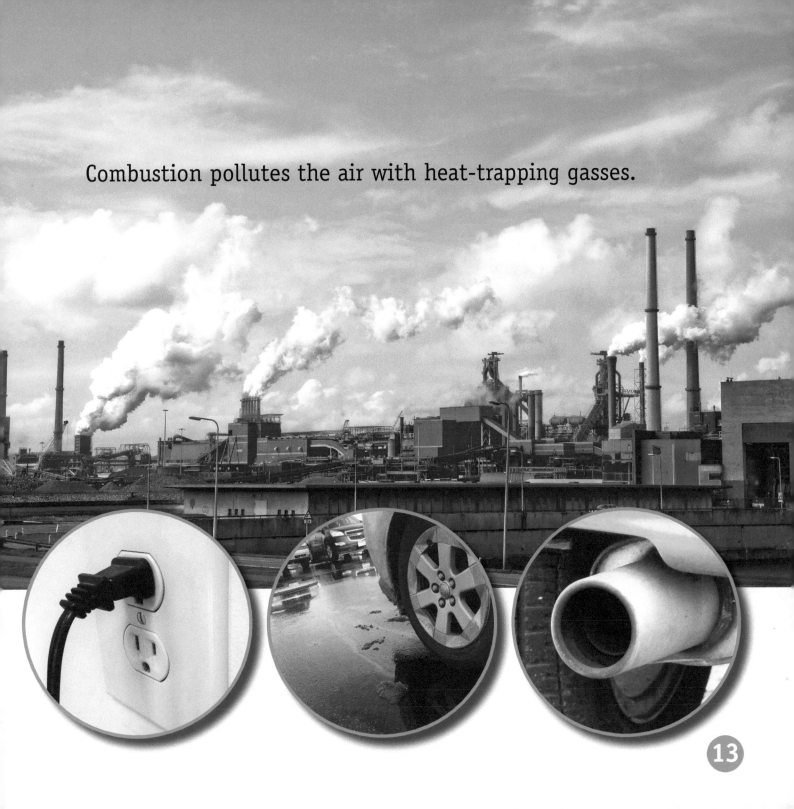

Lack of clean energy is a problem that needs solving. Let's work on it together.

What can you create to solve the problem?

5

C is for Climate.

Climate is the weather pattern over many years.
Some climates have 4 seasons each year:
winter, spring, summer, autumn.

Tropical climates have only 2 seasons:
wet season and dry season.

16

Our combustion habit, too many heat-trappers in the air, is changing climate everywhere.

6

C is for Connect.

Water, air, land, and living things are in us, around us, and through us. We are connected.

God is the source of all things.

19

How do you get around?

Biking, walking, bussing, and carpooling burn less
fuel. Less combustion is good for the air we share,
our climate, and God's creation.

20

Giveway to
Pedestrians

10

Six important C's to remember.

1. Creation
2. Christ
3. Creativity
4. Combustion
5. Climate
6. Connect

The 6 C's are around us everyday, we just need to look.

Which of the C words is your favorite?

How can we save energy and waste less? How do *you* use your creativity to care for Creation?

Glossary

Creativity: Making of new ideas or things

Creation: The environment around us near and far; land, air, water and living things

Combustion: Burning that puts heat-trapping gasses into the air

Climate: The weather pattern of a place over many years

Weather: The pressure, moisture, and temperature for one place at one moment